PRAISE FOR BRYCE THE THIRD AND THE HANDBOOK

Bryce the Third is a natural-born teacher and synthesizer of ideas. With *The Handbook*, he has seamlessly woven concepts from Stephen Covey and Oprah Winfrey with Hip Hop culture and New Thought to create an enjoyable read. *The Handbook* is an accessible and useful guide for writing your game plan for life success.
  John Anthony Majors, *Community Development Executive and Principal, The MIDAS Group*

The positivity Bryce The Third speaks shines a light and helps me to remember to look at situations with fresh eyes.
  Camille Zandbergen, *Lifelong Learner and Business Analyst*

With *The Handbook*, rap lyricist Bryce the Third deftly explores the enduring concepts of perception, gratitude, action, understanding, and completion with a depth that belies his age. What he offers us is his hard-earned bought wisdom.
  Dr. Tony Lamair Burks II, *Executive Coach and Author, Bought Wisdom: Tales of Living and Learning*

more...

Bryce The Third's reminders of integrity, as well as his consistent authenticity, has created a tidal wave of awakening in my life.
    Sema Melek, *Conscious Creator and Deep Breather*

I made a conscious effort to expand my world after the events of last year. Following Bryce The Third has opened my experiences to new places, people, and music. Hearing him speak about HIS struggles makes me realize that we are more alike than different.
    Joann Becker, *Wife, Mom, Grandma, and Jersey Girl*

The Handbook feels youthful to me and it is also perfect for anyone who wants to change their perspective.
    Willis W. Walker III, *Hospitality Strategist and Entrepreneur*

THE
HANDBOOK

BRYCE THE THIRD

Copyright © 2021 by R. Bryce Cobb III

No part of this publication may be reproduced, distributed, or transmitted in any form or by any means, including photocopying, recording, or other electronic or mechanical methods, without the prior written permission of the publisher, except in the case of brief quotations embodied in critical reviews and certain other noncommercial uses permitted by copyright law. All rights reserved.

Disclaimer: The contents of *The Handbook* are for informational purposes only. The content is not intended to be a substitute for professional advice, diagnosis, or treatment. Always seek the advice of your health professional or other qualified health provider with any questions, concerns, observations, or insights you may have regarding your health and wellness. Never disregard professional advice or delay in seeking it because of something you have read in *The Handbook*.

For permission requests, write to the publisher, Attention: Permissions Coordinator, at Brycethe3rd@gmail.com

"The Handbook" lyrics from the album, *Internal Revenue*, by Bryce The Third

Cover design by Pixel Studio

Printed and bound in the United States of America

The Handbook. / R. Bryce Cobb III. — 1st ed.
ISBN 978-1-954556-01-0

DEDICATION

This book is dedicated to my kiddos, Ryin Harmony Cobb and Bryce The Fourth. Let the fact that your Daddy is now an author be a testament that you can do ANYTHING you put your mind, heart, & focus to.

CONTENTS

Acknowledgments	i
Intro	iii
The Handbook Lyrics	vii
First Track: Perception	1
Second Track: Gratitude	11
Third Track: Action	19
Bonus Tracks	29
Understanding	35
Completion	43
Outro	51
About the Author	57
Engaging Bryce The Third	59
Index	61

ACKNOWLEDGMENTS

First and foremost, I want to thank Dr. Tony Lamair Burks II for helping me take the idea of my first book from conception to creation. This experience and your expertise have been invaluable. Thanks for letting me rent some of your bought wisdom.

To my Mom: Man, oh, man, what a blessing it has been to have you in my life. If no one believed in me, you damn sure did, every step of the way. From standing in the courtroom and not being able to hug each other to standing in the street back to back in a fist fight with five grown men, you've always had my back. I can't wait to chronicle our adventures thus far in the next book. Thank you for being my reference point for love.

To my Dad: From where we've come from to where we are has been a hell of a transformation. Thanks for always rooting for your boy.

To Sarah: To think that the conversation we had when I decided to pursue music for a year to see if something would shake would have led to me being an author, motivational speaker, mentor, coach and yet and still a fire ass rapper. Just wow. Thank you for all of your support and belief throughout the years.

To my Papa: "Popsicle" you have always been the loudest cheerleader of them all. This book you hold in your hands was written by that little Black boy you've always believed in. We're changing the world, Pop, and this is just the beginning! Those lottery tickets might never hit, but be sure that what you've invested in me will continue to yield returns!

To my siblings: Vash, Chloe, Christian & Raymo. WHATEVER WE WANT TO DO WE CAN DO IT! Your brother will continue to lead the way until his very last breath. I love you all more than words can express.

INTRO

"Think I'm through making the best out of bad situations. Think it's time to make the bad situations the best! "
 - Bryce The Third

I've always been hard pressed to identify with one specific thing. Coming up as a kid, I never really was able to fit in with one crowd. I'd be with the kids rapping in the hall one minute; then, I'd pop in on the skater crowd. I'd be on the soccer team and get out of practice and be all about video games. I used to consider it a weakness. Why can't I just choose one thing to be and stick to it like everybody else? When I made it to my adolescent years, that mindset caused me to hone in on one specific identity. "Hood Nigga." Let's just say that didn't work out either. That's for a whole 'nother book.

Fast forward to present day and what I used to consider a weakness is now one of my greatest strengths: multiple hats.

I AM a multitude of things.
I AM an avid reader.
I AM the CEO of *3 Feet Media*.
I AM paid to perform my music.
I AM a mentor to wayward youth.
I AM a recovery coach.
I AM a father.

And now as you read this book, I AM an author.

Let me give you a tiny peek into my multifaceted history as a preface to how this book came to be. Every now and then a couple of my "identities" leak into each other and form something new. Such is the case with *The Handbook*. *The Handbook* was originally a song I wrote and recorded in 2018 for my debut street album entitled *Internal Revenue*. The song detailed, at the time, what I had found to be dependable rules of thumb for living life. Fast forward a couple of years and I still agree with a good 90% of the song.

I've ALWAYS had a love for the English language and the art of communication. This was my reasoning for writing raps way back in 2002. Recently this love has led me to other forms of writing such as blog posts, articles, and scripts. I've DEFINITELY had the urge to write a book for a long time.

In a recent conversation with my cousin, Dr. Tony Lamair Burks II, an accomplished author himself, I told him it was a desire of mine to write a book. He suggested I take one of my songs and expound on some of its ideas. I could think of no other song than *The Handbook*. My music and my newfound love for long-form writing were about to collide.

In this book, I revisit and expound on *Perception*, *Gratitude*, and *Action*, three of the original four principles from *The Handbook*.

This book is designed to jumpstart your understanding of these three principles to get you moving towards your desired reality.

So what exactly is this book about? In short, it's about how to be a better person and live a more fulfilled existence. Throughout *The Handbook* I've compiled a few principles I carry with me and apply in my life on a daily basis. I have found over time that they have helped improve my quality of life. My productivity has increased and my present moment awareness is continuously evolving because I apply these principles. In moments of conflict and adversity, I have been able to apply one or all of these principles to get me not only over whatever it is, but THROUGH to the other side.

I've grown and become a responsible human being in the midst of applying these principles. I'm excited to share them with you so you may do the same! So buckle up and prepare to make a switch from trying to make the best out of bad situations, to dropping bad situations from your vocabulary and living nothing but the best!

Our first principle is the perfect place to begin this change.

Bryce The Third
October 2021

Disclaimer: The contents of *The Handbook* are for informational purposes only. The content is not intended to be a substitute for professional advice, diagnosis, or treatment. Always seek the advice of your health professional or other qualified health provider with any questions, concerns, observations, or insights you may have regarding your health and wellness. Never disregard professional advice or delay in seeking it because of something you have read in *The Handbook*.

THE HANDBOOK
by Bryce The Third

Sometimes I feel like I'm bout to lose my mind
but I know I gotta give it all I got/
Cuz I been through that door number one/
New journey has just begun,
said 'fail' then you bit your tongue/
Spoke 'lose'? Then you spit ya blood, fix ya mug.
Persistence./
Don't gotta guess what's the mission
Gon manifest in an instant./
But you gotta say it with your chest what you
mention./
Don't forget your intention/
I used to not could recognize./
Perception of deceptive eyes. But now I see.../
That I can have whatever I BELIEVE
that I can have and that's the policy/
The trick to that that I was missing,
"like attracting like" I'm now the prodigy/
So let me be the first to tell
you whatever you want,
first you gotta BE/

Now let's get it

Think I'm through making the best out of bad
situations!

Think it's time to make the bad situations the best!/

"How you do that?"

Well I'm glad that you asked me that question!
I made me a manual to pass
you can have for your quest/
Now this gon probably miss some niggas
but open your mind/
I can relate cuz as of now I'm still opening mine/
I wrote this rhyme to help you coax your mind to open
Hope in time it fix ya sight
to enlightenment from the broken kind/

Rule #1: Is very vital/
Compare it to the others most important gets the title/
The foundation if you aim to live a life of your conception/
Listen close cuz this a major key...
Nigga it's PERCEPTION!/
If you're rich or if you're broke, you're right...RIGHT NOW
Go and google 'paradigm'/
Basically the lens of which you see life through your pair of eyes/
Billionaire go broke he still a billionaire/
A lottery winner becomes a millionaire

they broke again within a year/

We all take in the same information/
But see what separates us is basic interpretation/
This what makes a racist racist and divides us as a nation/
But also brings us together depending on how you TAKE it/
Be aware what you perceive/
Only take in what's conducive to achieve/
Life a movie in which you depict the scenes/

(Do proceed)

Scrap your notions preconceived and let these supersede/
Only focus on the growth and let the stupid be/

Rule 2: be that mindset.
Thought alignment./
How you jumping off a building
you ain't even climb yet?/
You want better than you got you
gotta set the climate/
If you don't got it on your mind first
you'll never find it/
Short story to push the point further
Homeless man, he decides/
This no longer what he wanna be in life/
But he THINKS everyone with money

got that greed inside/
If you won't be the light
but you need the light
you won't see the light/

Rule 3: NOW THESE IN ORDER,
this where ACTION go/
You follow 1 and 2 know WHY you do
and WHAT you acting for/
This what make it happen though,
inspired action make it actual/
Know what you want, then act it out.
The universe'll back you though/
Which leads to 4…

Rule 4: oooh that's that gratitude!/
Be grateful when it comes,
AND IT'S GON COME
yeah that's that attitude!/
Be humble and love each other
don't you ever drop that oath/
I pray you never stop learning
and don't you ever stop your growth/

FIRST TRACK
PERCEPTION

per·cep·tion
/pərˈsepSH(ə)n/

> noun: perception; plural noun: perceptions
> - the ability to see, hear, or become aware of something through the senses. *"the normal limits to human perception"*
> - the state of being or process of becoming aware of something through the senses. *"the perception of pain"*
> - a way of regarding, understanding, or interpreting something; a mental impression. *"Hollywood's perception of the tastes of the American public"*

It's not what we see, It's HOW we see.
- Bryce The Third

Bryce The Third

What is your perception?

What if I told you the world begins and ends with you?
What if I told you the world began the moment you were born and will end as soon as you take your last breath?
Would you believe me?
Whether you agreed with me or not, you'd be right and that belief would shape how you continue to see the world.
Our minds and our hearts are like a pair of glasses through which we see everything.
For example, if in our hearts and minds we perceive the world to be a place of scarcity, a place full of hatred and misunderstanding, then that is what we will continue to see—and more than likely create—everywhere we go.
Now let's take off that proverbial pair of glasses and put on a pair that allows us to see a world of abundance, full of love and genuine connection. Likewise, we will start to see a world full of opportunities to love and to be loved. A world filled to the brim with exactly what we need exactly when we need it.

THE HANDBOOK

In this example, technically the world didn't change. What happened? We changed our perception and therefore the world as we used to see it no longer exists.

Imagine if you will a scenario in which a car runs into the back of a bus. In the aftermath of the accident you learned that an 80 year old passenger on the bus broke her leg in four places.

After reading the description of this event, how do you feel? Do you think the driver of the car should be held responsible for the damages?

Let's say that the 80 year old woman who was hurt in this incident just so happens to be your Grandmother? How do you feel about the driver of the car that hit that bus?

Ok, now let's broaden our view a bit.

Right before the accident between the car and the bus, a young mom was overwhelmed with a distressing conversation from work and let go of her two-year-old child's hand. As a result of this newfound freedom, the little girl runs away from mom fast, into the middle of the street, and directly into the path of an unsuspecting driver who instinctively swerves to avoid hitting the child. The result is the driver hits the back of the bus instead of hitting the two-year-old.

How do you feel NOW about the driver of the car with this newly acquired information? This is perception 101.

When all we knew was that a driver hit a bus our Grandma was on which led to a BELOVED member of our family going to the hospital with broken bones, we were most likely angry and wanted justice.

When we discovered that had not things played out the way they did, a child may have lost her life that day, our position may have shifted or softened.

This is the magic formula, the key to the kingdom, the *Secret Sauce*. Our perception changes once we gain more information.

Our entire life is made UP of events such as this. We begin interpreting things from the very moment we're born. We may never realize that our interpretation is just ONE way of looking at things. Often, what we call "Truth" is just an amalgamation of multiple instances of interpretation. We hardly stop to consider that there are 7.8

THE HANDBOOK

billion people on the planet interpreting things through different eyes. That's how we've come up with sayings like "That's just how life is" or "That's not how the world works" to which I would reply respectively, "WHO's life?" and "WHAT world?".

This information can be vital to those interested in making life bend to their will.

This information can be crucial to changing the course of your ENTIRE life.

Once we are aware of our power to discern what we label as *truth*, we gain the ability to change our outlook.

Close your eyes. When your eyes are closed, what do you see?

The world goes away for a bit, doesn't it? As soon as you reopen your eyes, the machine of perception begins to label things again. Blue sky. Tall building. Fast car. Brown skin. A perception bending exercise I practice often is to ask myself, "What would the blue sky be?" if I were never introduced to concepts such as colors? How does a blind person know what blue is? How do you teach a child who has never seen color what that specific color is? Who was the first person to decide that blue would be "blue"? Why do we continue to agree with them?

I know! I know it can seem a bit funny at first. Especially when talking about something as elementary as colors. But when we delve into more controversial institutions such as racism and poverty, our existence tends to bend a bit more.

Imagine growing up in a household and just as you were taught that the color blue was "blue", you were also taught that all brown people were different and not to be trusted. From the very moment you were born, this was your programming.

Now imagine the kid who grows up with this programming meeting a Brown kid for the first time at age 21. How do you think this kid will treat that person? It'll be counterintuitive and almost impossible for the kid to trust the Brown person or to see that person as equal. Such is the power of perception.

The beauty about becoming familiar with this process of perception is that once we learn how it works, we can switch off autopilot and become intentional about how

THE HANDBOOK

we see the world. Have you ever REALLY paid attention to the way you see the world? What are some beneficial outlooks on life that you have? What are some undesirable outlooks on life that you would change?

Use the next couple of pages to brainstorm about your current beliefs and how they serve you. Remember. NOTHING is set in stone. Change your mind and change the WORLD.

_____
_____
_____
_____
_____
_____
_____
_____
_____
_____
_____
_____
_____
_____
_____
_____

Bryce The Third

THE HANDBOOK

Bryce The Third

THE HANDBOOK

SECOND TRACK
GRATITUDE

grat i tude
/ˈɡradə₁t(y)o͞od/

> noun: gratitude
> - the quality of being thankful; readiness to show appreciation for and to return kindness. "she expressed her gratitude to the committee for its support"
> - a strong feeling of appreciation. "Our gratitude for the generous gift to the foundation was expressed in thoughtful letter to the new donor and in a letter to the editor of our local newspaper."

No matter what is going wrong in my life, there is always something going right.
 - Bryce The Third

What are you grateful for?

Always be GRATEFUL. Gratitude is the art of focusing on and appreciating what's good in life.

Gratitude, in my opinion, is an ARTFORM.

The ability to focus more on what's good than what's undesirable in life and the resulting creation of even more good deserves a black belt certification.

Have you ever been in the company of someone who is always complaining? The kind of person who is always spotlighting what is not going their way, someone whining about what they find undesirable?

Doesn't it seem like no matter what the circumstances, this person won't ever be happy or satisfied?

If it's raining it's "too wet" but if the sun is out it's "too bright to see".

Unfortunately, until this person changes their attitude towards life, they will continue to find and even create more things to be upset about.

THE HANDBOOK

I want to familiarize you with a concept called "confirmation bias".

By definition, confirmation bias is "the tendency to interpret new evidence as confirmation of one's existing beliefs or theories."

In essence, confirmation bias suggests that if you believe everything is trash and there is nothing good in the world, you will continue to find evidence to support your theory.

Now imagine if a person was appreciative of everything that came their way, whether it be sun or rain, joy, or pain. If confirmation bias is to be believed, then no matter what the circumstances are, this person will find something that makes life worthwhile and will continue to create a meaningful and fulfilling experience.

THIS is the power of gratitude.

Although gratitude can be defined as a feeling of equanimity, I want to put emphasis on gratitude as an ACTION. A lot of us don't come from an environment where intentionally spinning a situation—that on the outset may look bleak—into something that serves us is common practice. "I can't win for losing", "I can never get ahead," and "no good deed goes unpunished" are just a few of the poisonous sayings that are thrown around like it's nothing where I'm from.

    For the majority of us, at first, it will be counterintuitive to truly believe and speak into existence that things are actually working in our favor despite undesirable circumstances. The answer to that is to start with gratitude right where we are. We learn to say "thank you" for even the littlest of things that are going right. Upon further examination, we may even find that the littlest things are in fact the biggest blessings anyone could ask for.

    Am I breathing? Without breath, NOTHING would be possible because I wouldn't be ALIVE to make anything happen. Can I focus on my breath with an intense level of appreciation? How does it feel when I do this? Do I have access to my senses? Sight, smell, taste, touch, and sound. Not everybody does. If I do, I can be especially grateful to hear the sweet evening songs of the crickets at night or witness a magnificent sunset. There are SO many things

THE HANDBOOK

I can appreciate straight out the gate. We just have to learn how to hone in on these things with our focus.

The longer we're alive, the easier it is to take advantage of something we've always had access to such as a hug from another person. Nothing in life is promised or guaranteed. All it takes is something as novel as a virus like COVID19 to hit society and change our way of life and make hugs a thing of the past. When we learn to appreciate what we have, we'll learn that what we have is WAY bigger than we thought it was. It really is all we need. Even better, when we learn to have gratitude for what we have, we tune to a frequency that allows us to see more of what we've come to appreciate in the world.

In short, learn to love what you have, no matter what it is.

What are some things that you can be grateful for RIGHT NOW?

Don't use examples of things that you'll be grateful for once you accomplish or achieve them. I'm talking RIGHT NOW this very moment?

Bryce The Third

Use the next couple of pages to list them.

_____
_____
_____
_____
_____
_____
_____
_____
_____
_____
_____
_____
_____
_____
_____
_____
_____
_____
_____
_____
_____
_____
_____
_____

THE HANDBOOK

Bryce The Third

_____
_____
_____
_____
_____
_____
_____
_____
_____
_____
_____
_____
_____
_____
_____
_____
_____
_____
_____
_____

Come back to this section whenever you think of more things to add. Pull out this list and read it to yourself when you're in a bad mood or stuck in life.

THE HANDBOOK

THIRD TRACK
ACTION

action
/ ak-shuhn /

> noun: action
> - the process or state of acting or of being active *"The machine is not in action now."*
> - something done or performed; act; deed. *"the school board took action last night"*
> - an act that one consciously wills and that may be characterized by physical or mental activity *"Although she was bedridden she was moved to action; otherwise, she figured she'd wither away to nothing"*

"Words are just a manifestation of who we are and what we do. Prioritize taking action and let your moves speak volumes!"
- Bryce The Third

Bryce The Third

What action will you take today?

When I was coming up as a kid in the 90's, there was a huge slogan that you could not avoid. "Knowledge is power!"

Everywhere you'd go, every after school special on TV and every other episode of *Captain Planet* reaffirmed that knowledge is power. Well, years later and with a tiny bit of experience under my belt, I would have to disagree, at least partly.

I say knowledge alone is useless. But APPLIED knowledge, now that's where the true power lies! Imagine if you read this entire book and then when you were finished put it down and never put anything you learned from it to use! I know plenty of people who read a lot of books, and you'd be hard pressed to find any effects of what they've read in their lives. Don't be smart for the sake of being smart. Who can quote the most facts the fastest? To be honest, NOBODY CARES! What is important is that we take what we learn and we put it to use in our lives. Can we use what we know to support others on their respective journeys? We learn even more about ourselves when we serve as guides, mentors, wayshowers, and fellow sojourners for others. If we can take something we discover and apply it to our actual lives, that's when knowledge becomes WISDOM.

      Educated action. The balance of those two words is very intricate. We don't want to spend so much time researching and studying that we don't take action. There are some lessons that can only be learned once we take the first step and this is true across ALL endeavors. There is a concept called "analysis paralysis" that suggests we'll spend so much time analyzing something that it becomes close to impossible to even take the first step. There are lessons to be learned that we'll NEVER learn unless we take action NOW.

      However, it is VERY easy to confuse being 'busy' with being productive. If we don't take the time to educate ourselves, not only in our respective fields of practice but also on how we personally fit into those fields, we can potentially waste YEARS of our time and energy running around getting little to nothing actually accomplished.

Bryce The Third

At the end of the day, ACTION is king. Everybody has had a good idea but it's rare that a person FULLY acts on it. Only the person who is willing to take an idea from conception to completion can change the world. Nobody remembers the person who thought that a wheel could exist. Society only benefited from the one who actually INVENTED the wheel.

This is what weeds out people with potential from those who actually manifest their dreams. It takes a LOT to get something done. There will be tons of disappointment and people will doubt your ideas. Things that seemed as if they would work on paper, will fail in implementation. It will be back to the drawing board over and over. The world changers; however, persist and continue to take action. People who affect REAL change grasp on to the previous rules of well-trained perception and an immense sense of gratitude and push boundaries in the face of adversity. The key to doing a good job is to DO a good job. Show up, take educated action, learn from your mistakes, iterate, and act some more!

THE HANDBOOK

Never stop pushing for what you believe.

What are some ideas that you've been wanting to act on but haven't for whatever reason? Why haven't you? Do you think the idea is silly? Did you tell somebody your idea and in turn they made you feel like it was a dumb idea? (*Side Note:* no idea is dumb and you 100% told the wrong person). Set a timer for 8 minutes and flip to the next few pages. Jot down as many ideas as you can think of that have been tossed away. No idea is too big or too small. Put it all down. Once the timer is up circle the top 8 ideas that call to your spirit the most. Live with those ideas for 24 hours then choose the one out of that top 8 that calls to you the most.

I challenge you to act on this ONE idea and bring it to fruition! Breathe life into this one idea...and then repeat until you've done the same with the rest of the 7 ideas. And then return to these pages, set the time for another 8 minutes and write down whatever comes up for you, remembering that there are no dumb ideas. Then, once again, circle the top 8 ideas that call to your spirit the most. Marinate on those ideas for 24 hours then choose the ONE idea that calls your name the most. I recommend going through this process at least once each season: winter, spring, summer, and fall.

_____
_____
_____
_____
_____
_____
_____
_____
_____
_____
_____
_____
_____
_____
_____
_____
_____
_____
_____

THE HANDBOOK

Bryce The Third

THE HANDBOOK

Bryce The Third

THE HANDBOOK

BONUS TRACKS

bo ·nus track
/ˈbōnəs trak/

> noun: bonus track
> - a piece of music which has been included as an extra; a special listing or recording found on CD or vinyl albums. *"His debut album was remastered and reissued in 2006 with an exclusive bonus track."*

A bonus track can be the cherry on top of the sundae of an already classic album."
- Bryce The Third

Bryce The Third

What are the bonus tracks of your life?

This book is such a marriage between my music and my love for writing that I think it would be an injustice to not have some "Bonus Tracks". Some of my favorite albums have what is called a hidden or bonus track.

For those of you who are unfamiliar with the concept of bonus tracks on an album, bonus tracks are the songs that weren't necessarily meant to be on the album originally. Sometimes an artist will include these songs on the deluxe edition of an album to entice a customer to pay a couple of extra dollars. Lucky you! I'm going to include a couple of extra principles here in these pages for free!

I released *Internal Revenue*, the street album that's the source material for this book in 2018. I wrote the song, *The Handbook,* maybe a half of a year before that. Needless to say, quite a bit of time has elapsed since I wrote the song. Time and I have quite the relationship. In this instance, in the amount of time since I first wrote the song, I've had an insane amount of life experience.

THE HANDBOOK

In my experience, I have learned that time doesn't guarantee me growth. It does; however, allow me the opportunity to turn my experience into wisdom that serves me. Let's be honest, you can be a very ignorant 75 year old if you choose to squander the opportunity to use time to your advantage. The only difference between an 8 year old and a 60 year old is the time that they've been allowed to roam the earth and the potential to learn from mistakes and garner wisdom that comes with those experiences. Potential is the key word here. The fulfillment of potential is solely based on the willingness of an individual to work towards their fulfillment. In simple terms, you don't get shit for just being here. There are no participation trophies in life.

Anyways, in the time since I wrote *The Handbook*, I have been putting in WORK. Emotionally, spiritually, physically, financially, and any of the other "allys" you can think of. In the words of The Notorious Biggie Smalls, "things done changed."

The beauty of growth, in my experience, is that we never know what we're going to grow into. I couldn't have imagined that I'd be writing a book, based on a song I wrote and that you would have it in your hands right now and be reading it...but here we are. I NEVER would have imagined that I'd be giving guided meditations or mentoring youth or producing documentaries either but...well, you get the idea.

There is an adage I once heard that resonates beautifully in my soul, "You can't open a flower with a sledgehammer". The unfolding of who we are to become can only come from patient curiosity and the determination to be shown. Over and over, we must show up ready to do the work and like the flower, learn to bloom at the pace of life. We might have to learn to be OK with the fact that what we bloom into might not look like what we thought it would. We might have to be open to blossoming into a species of flower we've never seen.

I'm giving you a bit of background behind my growth because I feel that I've learned a few things in my experience that might serve as a substantial addition to the original principles in *The Handbook*. The perfect "bonus tracks" for the occasion.

THE HANDBOOK

These *Bonus Tracks* are straight up about TRANSFORMATION. Don't stress over what "they" might say about you and how you've changed and grown. I mean, change is really the only way you'll get the most out of this book and YOUR life.

Use the next couple of pages to vibe on these: What are some things that have changed about you over the last few years? How are you different? What sets the "you of back then" apart from the "you of today"?

_____
_____
_____
_____
_____
_____
_____
_____
_____
_____
_____
_____

Bryce The Third

THE HANDBOOK

BONUS TRACK
UNDERSTANDING

un·der·stand·ing
/ˌəndərˈstandiNG/

> noun: understanding adjective: understanding
> - the ability to understand something; comprehension *"She has a clear understanding of our expectations."*
> - sympathetically aware of other people's feelings; tolerant and forgiving *"The new counselor is very understanding."*

Habit 5: Seek First to Understand, Then to Be Understood
- Stephen Covey *"The 7 Habits of Highly Effective People"*

Bryce The Third

How do you seek understanding?

It's crazy as I sit here and write this book. I–lowkey–did not remember where I first heard this quotation. The order of operation that is seeking to understand and THEN to be understood has become such a part of my DNA at this point that until a Google search revealed Stephen Covey had TRADEMARKED the phrase, I might've told you that I came up with it!

    For me, understanding has to be applied on a daily basis. Interaction after interaction for me to be my best self, I have to seek to understand where others are coming from. There are a LOT of different people on this planet and they all come from different backgrounds. I'm one of these people. All of the things I've seen and the experiences I've had and the people I've met and the places I've been make up the person who is writing these words right now. Why would I EVER assume that when presented with another person who has had different experiences, seen different things, and been to different places that we would immediately see eye to eye on everything we've individually come to understand the world to be?

Earlier we've touched a bit on what we are about to discuss now in *Track One: PERCEPTION*. Remember the story about growing up and being taught that the color blue was "blue"? Now imagine if someone was taught that what you have come to identify as the color blue was "green". The process of understanding allows us to try our best to see how someone could have landed on a conclusion that differs from our own. Most times when someone disagrees with us, it's easy to find the other person's point of view absurd. "How in the world can blue be green??" We'd say. "It's blue!!!" Seeking to understand a person's point of view that differs from our own can oftentimes feel counterintuitive but through this process I've discovered just how insubstantial some of my OWN ideas are. Seeking to understand and being willing to admit that I might not know as much as I thought I knew, paradoxically, has led to me learning some pretty cool things.

Do you remember the PEMDAS method from math class? You know the acronym that helped us to remember the order of operations for math problems. Parentheses, Exponents, Multiplication, Division, Addition and subtraction, in that order. PEMDAS! It's an acronym that became the mnemonic phrase, "Please Excuse My Dear Aunt Sally". It was sort of a formula for me. If a problem had addition, parentheses, and multiplication elements and you tried to solve by doing the addition first, you would end up solving with an incorrect answer.
Seeking to understand and THEN to be understood operates in a similar manner. It is a FORMULA and it puts things in a specific order for a reason.

On the "Pivotal-to-My-Growth-as-an-Individual" scale, the *Seeking Understanding* portion of the formula trumps the *Being Understood* portion all day long and twice on Sunday! Not everyone has the capacity or the maturity to put this formula into effect, therefore it is of the UTMOST importance that you, someone who HAS the capacity, prioritize being patient and understanding with those who don't. Sound fair? No? Welp, life is a lot of things but "fair" isn't something I see it as often being. It's on US to be understanding of people who may not have the capacity to be understanding of us. If you seek a life of growth, free from resentment and judgement, it just is what it is. It is very reminiscent of the adage, "If you knew better, you'd do better" As you are reading these words you are being equipped to know better than a majority of the human population. Now you gotta do better, baby!

    Seeking understanding without the promise of being understood in return may seem like an unfair, burdensome task. "If they won't take the time to understand where I'm coming from then why in the world should I give a rats ass about anything they have to say?!?" you may ask. I hear you and I completely understand; but, hear me out because the upside to this practice is immeasurable. Riches beyond your current comprehension lie ahead if you can just set aside what it is you feel you currently know and be open to having the willingness to understand someone else's point of view.

Even if after seeking to understand, you find that you still disagree, you've done what a huge chunk of humans can not do. You've taken the time to get outside of yourself. To double check to see if what you've come to know as facts are in fact facts. This, my friend, is exactly where perpetual growth lies. If perception is the key to the kingdom, then the practice of seeking to understand is like the skeleton key to all of the kingdoms in the world.

Use the next couple of pages to reflect on these: When's the last time you simply didn't understand something and that lack of understanding created a problem or a challenge? What was the misunderstanding or lack of understanding really about? If you could redo that moment what would you change?

_____
_____
_____
_____

THE HANDBOOK

Bryce The Third

THE HANDBOOK

BONUS TRACK
COMPLETION

com ple tion
/kəmˈplēSH(ə)n/

> noun: completion
> - the action or process of finishing something
> - the state of being finished "the completion of the project before his promotion to manager was important to Ronald"

"Success is completion. Success is being able to complete what we set out to do - each individual action, each specific step, each desired experience whether a big project or a very small errand."
- Susan Collins

Bryce The Third

What is the importance of completion?

As this book officially comes to a close (no more bonus tracks I promise), I think it's the perfect time for me to harp on the importance of finishing things. I know, I know. It's not "perfect" yet. You don't want to put it out. You feel it can be better. I want to let you in on a little secret though. "Perfect" doesn't exist.

That's right, perfection is a fib. "It needs to be perfect first" is the beautiful lie that we tell ourselves which in most circumstances shrouds the truth of the matter which is that we are SCARED. Whatever it is, do it and do it all the way.

There aren't too many feelings as overwhelming as having the ghosts of past unfinished and unreleased projects floating over your shoulder. This burden makes it impossibly difficult to start the next endeavor. Often if an unfinished project preceded the one that I'm about to begin, the newest project suffers immensely, if I even finish the project at all.

THE HANDBOOK

Take your ideas, work on them thoroughly; but, most importantly, learn when to wrap it up. The beauty in this is that as long as we continue to breathe we can create some more. We can always express more ideas in the next project.

It never fails that no matter how 'perfect' I thought something I made was in the moment, in hindsight, I always notice something I could have done better. In other words, no matter how much energy and effort you put into what it is you are creating, the further you get from the moment you created it, the more you'll see you could have done better. So since this'll always be the case, just do it. It doesn't have to be perfect and as a matter of fact it never will!
Get it done!

With all this said—well, at least written—let's get a bit meta. That is, let's go deeper and reflect. I always knew in my heart of hearts that I'd write a book. I've talked about it with others, thrown ideas around, and contemplated the subject matter for a couple years now. It wasn't until the encouragement of Dr. Tony Lamair Burks II that I put the principles and ideas from the previous Track on ACTION into play.

The question begs to be asked though, "What if I took the initial action of getting started but never actually FINISHED this book?" If I never took this idea from conception all the way through to creation, you wouldn't be holding anything in your hand right now. In my opinion that would be a tragedy, especially if you've read anything at all in this book that has helped you or brought about an epiphany that may lead to change.

I think it's good to become familiar with some of the reasons we may start but never complete so that we can identify when these things are in play:

- **Self-doubt** can slip in right when you least expect it to do so. It's older cousin "self-sabotage" is also waiting in the wings to pounce on you and your divine ideas and projects.

- **Limiting beliefs** about your idea or project midway through. It's that sinking feeling of "Am I smart enough?" "Will I fall flat on my face and look stupid?"

- **Discouragement** from others. Think about it, many times we share our ideas and projects with those who simply don't understand what we are seeking to accomplish. They don't or can't understand your vision.
- **Obstacles and adversity** are inevitable when our ideas become projects. What you choose to do when you encounter obstacles and adversity will determine your ultimate success.
- **Fear of negative reception** of what it is we are creating: "Will people like this?" and much more.

On the *Third Track: Action*, I asked you to think about some ideas that you've been wanting to act on but haven't for whatever reason. Then I asked you to jot down as many ideas as you can think of that have been tossed away. Then I asked you to work on one just one idea. Now is there one idea from your list that you've been avoiding like the plague? The one that you really should be working on. Yeah, that one! Use the next couple of pages to reflect on that one idea and how you can bring it to completion.

_____
_____
_____
_____
_____
_____
_____
_____
_____
_____
_____
_____
_____
_____
_____
_____
_____
_____
_____
_____
_____
_____
_____

THE HANDBOOK

Bryce The Third

THE HANDBOOK

OUTRO

The more I learn, the more I realize how much I don't know. - Albert Einstein

The outcome I hope for you is that as a result of reading this book, you are able to find inspiration to get started right here and now. Now that you are at the stage of acting on your ideas, theoretically, the cycle continues. It's as simple or as complex as you allow it to be. The three rules of *The Handbook* work in order, together, perpetually. And I do mean forever, forever, ever.

When we are constantly aware of the state of our perception, we are empowered to break out of our "normal" (*Perception*). Being aware of how we perceive life is the Secret Sauce that perpetually allows us to see ourselves, each other, and our world with fresh eyes. When we learn to be grateful for what we see with those eyes, we find satisfaction and peace *(Gratitude)*. In a state of peace, our spirits are naturally filled to the brim with creativity. We'll start to envision a world in which we are supported every step of the way. It is at this point that we use our faith and creativity to take action on what we believe *(Action)*.

Forever be willing to see with new eyes. Be grateful for what it is we see. Take action on our ideas. Repeat ad infinitum.

Perception and gratitude precede action because most times the battle of life is either won or lost before we even enter the ring. It is SO very important that we have the right attitude before we take action because our mindset determines how productive we'll actually be. When we make the inevitable mistake, the right perception will align us with the lesson embedded in our failure. Gratitude will pick us back up on our feet because although we may have taken a loss, we still have so many things to be grateful for. We dust ourselves off and get right back to being and acting in a way that brings us closer to our goals.

I've personally learned that the growth that comes as a result of putting these principles to work is everlasting. As long as we put in the work, we will continue to elevate in understanding of ourselves and our environments.

I have; however, through putting these principles to work, stumbled across a life mission. My mission is to spread a message of hope, responsibility, and self accountability through art, conversation, and media. Living this mission has brought me joy and challenge; at times it has been a rough, uphill road. Creating content, gaining attention, being consistent, self funding projects, improving, and iterating constantly can be VERY energy consuming. I love every minute of it though! This is the most fulfilled I've been yet, in my life, and my capacity for this work continues to grow. I owe all of this to the principles that I've outlined for you in this book.

Bryce The Third

I leave you with the same sentiment that I left listeners with on the song that became this book:

> "Be humble and love each other. Don't you ever drop that oath.
> I pray you never stop learning and don't you ever stop your growth!"

I'm gone.

Disclaimer: The contents of *The Handbook* are for informational purposes only. The content is not intended to be a substitute for professional advice, diagnosis, or treatment. Always seek the advice of your health professional or other qualified health provider with any questions, concerns, observations, or insights you may have regarding your health and wellness. Never disregard professional advice or delay in seeking it because of something you have read in *The Handbook*.

THE HANDBOOK

Bryce The Third

ABOUT THE AUTHOR

Bryce Ronald Cobb III (*Bryce The Third*) is a rap lyricist, coach, writer, and an entrepreneur. He writes, performs and produces hip hop cooked in soul based on his evocative urban poetry. What began as a foray into the rap music industry became much more. Music connected him with his love for communication. This connection sparked an evolution that enabled him to touch souls in many ways. From instagram posts and podcast appearances to YouTube videos and albums, he harnesses the power of media to offer different points of view and ignite change and growth.

A certified peer recovery mentor (CPRM), he has been a student and practitioner of personal development since beginning his own road to recovery in 2013. He is the founder of *3 Feet Media* and *Rough But Worth It Recovery* where he leverages his lived experiences, craft knowledge, and the wisdom he's cultivated to help others.

Raised by a single mother, he became a father at 16. He battled drug addiction before ditching his demons and dedicating himself to his craft. He is passionate about supporting people in discovering their personal strength and potential as they become accountable for their own lives. He doesn't operate in a world where you "do one thing to do it well". He does what he wishes as he pursues the desires of his heart. His purpose is to plant seeds that unlock your growth potential as an individual so that you may live a life of transformation and abundance.

AMAZON REVIEWS

If this book has impacted you in ANY way, please leave a review on Amazon!

This is THE most impactful way for independent authors to gain exposure and to help others discover the good info you've found in our books.

Besides buying this book, leaving an Amazon Review is the BEST way you can support!

Thanks a ton,
  'Til next time
    - Bryce The Third

ENGAGING BRYCE THE THIRD

Bryce The Third is a mental and emotional wellness mentor teaching you the tools for building a healthy mental, emotional, and spiritual foundation. This solid foundation paves the way, empowering you to tackle with confidence anything life throws at you.

Work with *Bryce The Third* to step-by-step create the life and relationships of your dreams that you desire unlike you've ever imagined. 1-on-1 mentoring available by special request hitme@brycethethird.com

Check out *"You Feel That?" with Bryce The Third* on your favorite podcast platform. *Bryce The Third* is also available for:

- Speaking Engagements
- Workshops and Seminars
- Music and Entertainment

Follow him on his social media platforms. Give him a shout. Check out his online course offerings.

www.BryceTheThird.com
Instagram: @BryceTheThird
Facebook: Bryce The Third
YouTube: youtube.com/BryceTheThird

INDEX

3 Feet Media, 57

Action, 13, 19-22, 36, 38, 43, 46-47, 52
Aware, 1, 5, 35, 51

Bryce The Third, 1, 11, 19, 29, 57, 59
Burks II, Tony Lamair, 45

Change, 3-5, 7, 12, 15, 22, 31, 33, 40, 46, 57

Einstein, Albert, 51
Exercise, 5

Gratitude, 11-15, 22, 52
Growth, 31-32, 38-40, 53-54, 57-58

Handbook, The, 30-32, 51
Human, 1, 39-40

Ideas, 22-24, 37, 45-47, 51-52

Knowledge, 20-21, 57

Life, 4-5, 7, 11-13, 15, 18, 23, 30-33, 39, 51-53, 58
Love, 2, 4, 15, 30, 53-54, 57

Mindset, 52
Music, 29-30, 57, 59

Perception, 1-6, 22, 37, 40, 48, 51-52

Perfect, 32, 44-45
Principles, 30-32, 46, 53

Smalls, The Notorious Biggie, 31

Think, 3, 6, 18, 23, 30-31, 44, 46-47

Understanding, 1-2, 35-40, 53

Work, 3, 5-6, 14, 22, 31-32, 45, 47, 51, 53, 59

Made in the USA
Monee, IL
29 January 2024